The Power of
PRAYING®
for Your
Adult Children

STORMIE
OMARTIAN

HARVEST HOUSE PUBLISHERS
EUGENE, OREGON

**THE POWER OF PRAYING® FOR YOUR ADULT CHILDREN
PRAYER AND STUDY GUIDE**
Copyright © 2009, 2014 by Stormie Omartian
Published by Harvest House Publishers
Eugene, Oregon 97408
www.harvesthousepublishers.com

ISBN 978-0-7369-5796-0 (pbk.)
ISBN 978-0-7369-5797-7 (eBook)

Printed in the United States of America

20 21 22 / BP-JH / 10 9 8 7

This book belongs to

_____

*Please do not read beyond this page
without permission of the person named above.*

A supplemental workbook to
The Power of Praying for Your Adult Children
by Stormie Omartian,
for anyone interested in practical
group or individual study.

Contents

How Do I Begin?

I'm sure you already know that as a parent you never stop being concerned about your adult children. And I am also sure that this is exactly why you are reading this book—because you want to pray for your adult children powerfully enough to make a big difference in their lives. Well, the best way I know to do that is to deepen your own relationship with the Lord so you can enjoy greater power in your prayers. In order for that to happen, you need to study the Word of God, which will strengthen you, help you grow in faith, and give you a better understanding of who God is and what He wants to do in your adult children's lives as well as your own. I don't mean that you will necessarily know all the details of their lives and everything they are dealing with, but you *will* have greater insight from God's perspective as to how to pray effectively for them. Also, I want to help you make a habit of fortifying your prayers with Scripture, because this is a powerfully effective and excellent tool. This *Prayer and Study Guide* will help you to do all of the things I have mentioned above as you respond to every question or direction in each chapter. In the process you will also find the peace of mind God has for you, which you must have no matter what you or your adult children are facing.

What You Will Need

This *Prayer and Study Guide* is divided into a 15-week plan for use in personal or group study. You will need to have my book, *The*

Power of Praying for Your Adult Children to read along with this. The answers to many questions will be found in it. You will also need a Bible. I have referred to the New King James Version here, but you can use whatever translation you want. Just make sure the Bible you use is easy for you to understand.

How to Proceed

In group study, it is good to follow the order of this book so that everyone will literally be on the same page when you come together each week. In individual study, you do not have to proceed in order if you have pressing concerns that need to be prayed about immediately. However, whether you are in a group or reading this *Prayer and Study Guide* by yourself, go through the first four weeks in order before you do any of the others. The reason for this is that they are the foundation for all of the other chapters, and everything will progress more smoothly if these four areas are covered in prayer first. You will see what I mean when you get into it.

In a Group

When studying in a group, read the assigned chapter for the week in *The Power of Praying for Your Adult Children* and answer the questions in the corresponding chapter here in the *Prayer and Study Guide* on your own. When the group comes together, the leader will go over the questions and discuss what insights God has given each person as he or she feels led to share them. This will be a perfect time to pray as a group for your adult children. Group intercession is very powerful, so don't pass up the opportunity to do so. You don't have to share in detail about your child because, as an adult, he or she deserves privacy. But if there is a serious situation, I wouldn't hesitate to share whatever is necessary in order to tap into the power of group prayer, especially if it will rescue your son or daughter from dire consequences. Ask God to give you wisdom about that.

All that being said, each of these chapters are about preventative prayer as well as restorative prayer. Your child doesn't have to have a problem in any of these areas in order to pray that he or she will not have one in the future. Every area of prayer focus mentioned in this book applies to anyone, and the prayers at the end of each chapter can be prayed over any adult child at any age.

The answering of each question that is of a personal nature is private and for your eyes only. The purpose of these questions is to help you determine your prayer focus and to better understand your own feelings about that subject as it relates to your adult children. Don't feel you *must* share the answers to these questions with the group unless you feel specifically led to do so for the purpose of group prayer or to help someone else better understand how to pray. The answers to the Bible-based questions are always good to share with one another—especially with regard to how those Scriptures enriched, enlightened, or fortified you, and how they influenced your prayers.

Your Role as an Intercessor for Your Adult Child

An intercessor prays for someone and makes it possible for that person to have a greater ability to respond to God. When you pray for your adult child, that makes you an intercessor for his or her life. It doesn't give *you* power *over* them, but it invites *God* to show His power *toward* them. No one else will ever intercede for your adult children with the fervency and consistency that you will. That's why your prayers of faith will have the power to affect their lives. And your knowledge of the Word of God that you will gain in this study and include in your prayers will help you to pray in greater faith so you can see amazing results. This prayer and Bible study is a wonderful opportunity to affect the lives of your adult children for eternity, as well as here and now.

WEEK ONE

Read the Introduction: "What Every Parent of an Adult Child Needs to Know" in *The Power of Praying for Your Adult Children*

Also read Chapter 1: "Pray That Your Adult Children Will See God Pour Out His Spirit upon Them." (This is the longest reading assignment in the *Prayer and Study Guide*, but it is important to establish a strong foundation for both you and your adult children in the beginning.)

1. Of the SEVEN THINGS EVERY PARENT OF AN ADULT CHILD NEEDS TO KNOW (found on pages 6-30 in *The Power of Praying for Your Adult Children*, from here on known as "the book"), were there any that you especially needed to hear? Perhaps you suspected some of them, but you didn't know for certain. Or you knew these things all along, but it helped you to hear it from someone else as well. Or perhaps you have never realized any of this before. It's important to come to terms with each of these truths, so explain your reaction to each one below.

Truth 1—You Need to Know It Never Ends: Do you believe that being a parent of an adult child never ends and that you always have a responsibility to pray for him or her? How do you feel about that challenge? (See pages 6-9 in the book.) Explain.

_____

_____

_____

_____

_____

_____

Truth 2—You Need to Know You Can't Fix Them: Do you believe that you can't "fix" your adult children? How do you feel about that? Does knowing this free you from feeling that you must try to do something to change them? (See pages 9-11 in the book.) Explain.

_____

_____

_____

_____

_____

_____

_____

_____

Truth 3—You Need to Know God Can Change Everything: Do you believe that God can change things in your adult child's life in response to prayer? Do you believe without a doubt that God will hear your prayers for your adult children and can deliver you from any fear you have concerning them? Do you believe that God is greater than your adult child's needs and that your prayers have power? (See pages 12-16 in the book.) Explain.

_____

_____

_____

_____

_____

_____

Truth 4—You Need to Know You Must Stop Blaming Yourself: Do you believe that you must stop blaming yourself for anything that has gone wrong in your adult child's life? Are there ways in which you blame yourself for things that have happened—or have *not* happened—to any one of your adult children? (See pages 16-19 in the book.) Explain.

_____

_____

_____

_____

_____

Truth 5—You Need to Know You Have to Forgive: Do you believe that you must forgive your adult children for anything they may have done to hurt or disappoint you? Do you need to forgive your adult child's other parent(s) for anything, as well as forgive anyone who has hurt your adult child? Do you believe you need to forgive yourself for any way in which you feel you could have been a better parent? Are any of these a challenge for you right now? (See pages 19-25 in the book.) Explain.

_____

_____

_____

_____

_____

_____

_____

_____

_____

Truth 6—You Need to Know There Is Only One Perfect Parent: Do you believe that there has only been one perfect parent and that it is our Father God? Do you find it easy or difficult to relate to God as your heavenly Father? (See pages 25-27 in the book.) Explain.

_____

_____

_____

_____

_____

_____

Truth 7—You Need to Know You Can Wholeheartedly Say, "For This *Adult* Child I Prayed": Do you believe that you have thoroughly covered your adult children in prayer in the past? If so, how have you seen answers to your prayers? If not, write out a prayer asking God to help you learn to pray in power for them from now on. (See pages 27-30 in the book.)

_____

_____

_____

_____

_____

_____

2. Have you ever dedicated your child to God? If not, write out the prayer of dedication found on page 28, second paragraph, in the book. If you have already dedicated your child to God in the past, write out the prayer of rededication to God that is found on page 28, third paragraph. Add your own words as you would like.

_____

_____

_____

_____

_____

_____

_____

3. Do you trust God enough to release your adult child (children) into His hands? If so, write out a prayer doing exactly that. If not, write out a prayer telling God how you feel about doing that and why. Ask Him to help you entrust them into His care.

    _____

    _____

    _____

    _____

    _____

    _____

    _____

    _____

    _____

    _____

4. Read the following Scriptures. What do the promises of God contained within these verses mean to you as a praying parent of an adult child? Write your answer in the space below.

    1 John 5:14-15

    _____

    _____

    _____

    _____

    _____

Matthew 7:7-8

_____

_____

_____

_____

_____

Ephesians 3:20-21

_____

_____

_____

_____

5. Pray the prayer on page 31 in the book. Include any specifics
   about yourself as a parent and your relationship with each of
   your adult children that you want God to hear from your heart.
   Write them out below.

   _____

   _____

   _____

   _____

   _____

   _____

6. Read Luke 11:11-13. In the two verses prior to verses 11-13, Jesus makes it clear that God wants us to keep praying—that is, keep "asking," "seeking," and "knocking." And the reason He does is because He wants to give good gifts to His children. If earthly fathers give good gifts to their children, how much more will our heavenly Father give good things to us—*His* children—when we ask Him? What is the gift mentioned here in verse 13 that is the greatest gift our heavenly Father will give us when we ask?

   _____

   _____

   How much would you do for your adult children if they asked you to do something for them? Do you believe that *God* would do as much for them? Would He do as much for *you*?

   _____

   _____

   _____

   _____

   _____

   _____

7. Read Acts 1:8. What does an outpouring of the Holy Spirit bring into your life?

   _____

   God wants to give His power to those who seek it in their lives. He wants to share His power with us so it is released into situations and lives when we ask for it in prayer. God wants you to invite Him to work in power in your adult children's lives. How would you especially like to see the power of the Holy Spirit move in your adult children's lives today?

_____

_____

_____

_____

_____

_____

8. Read Acts 2:38-39. What is the requirement that must be fulfilled before receiving the gift of the Holy Spirit?

_____

_____

_____

_____

    To whom was this promise made? Does that include you and your adult children?

_____

_____

_____

9. Read the following Scriptures, and beside each one write down what gift or blessing the Holy Spirit can bring to your adult child's life.

John 16:13

_____

_____

_____

Luke 12:12

_____

_____

_____

1 Corinthians 2:12

_____

_____

_____

Romans 15:13

_____

_____

_____

1 Corinthians 12:3

_____

_____

_____

John 14:26

_____

_____

_____

Romans 5:5

_____

_____

_____

Ephesians 1:13-14

_____

_____

_____

10. Pray the prayer on pages 40-41 in the book. What other requests for your adult child would you like to include in this prayer? Write them out below.

_____

_____

_____

_____

_____

WEEK TWO

Read Chapter 2: "Pray That Your Adult Children Will
Develop a Heart for God, His Word, and His Ways"
from *The Power of Praying for Your Adult Children*

1. Read the following Scriptures. According to each verse, why is
   it important for your adult child to have a relationship with the
   Lord? Write out your answers in the spaces below.

   Acts 3:19

   _____

   _____

   _____

   _____

   _____

   Acts 4:12

   _____

   _____

   _____

   _____

   _____

2 Corinthians 5:17

_____
_____
_____
_____

2 Peter 3:9

_____
_____
_____
_____

John 1:12

_____
_____
_____
_____

John 10:9

_____
_____
_____
_____

Write out a prayer asking God to draw your adult child to Himself to either begin a relationship with Him (if your adult child does not know the Lord), or to renew and *deepen* an existing relationship with the Lord (if your adult child has already received the Lord).

_____

_____

_____

_____

_____

_____

_____

_____

2.   Read 2 Chronicles 16:9. What blessing does God have for those who have a heart for Him?

_____

_____

_____

_____

_____

3.   Read James 4:8. What does God promise those who draw near to Him with their hearts?

_____

_____

Write out a prayer for your adult children that they will draw near to God so that He will be near to them.

_____

_____

_____

_____

_____

_____

4. Read John 16:7-8. According to these verses, how can we live the way we are supposed to? (Jesus is referring to the Holy Spirit here as our Helper.)

_____

_____

_____

_____

Read Romans 8:5-8. In light of this section of Scripture, how are we supposed to live? How, then, should you pray for your adult child to live?

_____

_____

_____

_____

5. Read the Scriptures below. According to these verses, why does your adult child need to have a heart for God's Word?

John 15:7

_____

_____

_____

_____

_____

Psalm 19:7-8

_____

_____

_____

_____

_____

Proverbs 13:13-14

_____

_____

_____

_____

_____

In light of the Scriptures above, how could you pray for your adult children? Write out your answer as a prayer using some of the words from these verses.

_____

_____

_____

_____

_____

_____

_____

_____

6. According to the Scriptures below, why does your adult child need to have the fear of God in his or her heart?

Proverbs 19:23

_____

_____

_____

_____

Psalm 145:19

_____

_____

_____

_____

Psalm 25:14

_____

_____

_____

_____

_____

Proverbs 29:25

_____

_____

_____

_____

Proverbs 1:28-29

_____

_____

_____

_____

Psalm 34:9-10

_____

_____

_____

_____

Proverbs 22:4

_____

_____

_____

_____

_____

Proverbs 16:6

_____

_____

_____

_____

_____

Keeping the Scriptures above in mind, write out a prayer for your adult children asking God to put the fear of the Lord in their hearts. (For example, "Lord, I pray that (names of adult children) will have the fear of the Lord and a reverence for You so that they will not be visited with evil...")

_____

_____

_____

_____

_____

_____

7. In light of the following Scriptures, in what ways could you pray in order to affect the state of your adult child's heart? Write out your answer as a short prayer under each reference. (For example, "Lord, I pray that You would give (<u>name of adult child</u>) a heart that can receive correction...")

Jeremiah 5:3-4

_____

_____

_____

_____

_____

_____

_____

Matthew 22:37

_____

_____

_____

_____

_____

_____

_____

_____

John 7:38

_____

_____

_____

_____

_____

_____

_____

Matthew 6:21

_____

_____

_____

_____

_____

Psalm 119:2

_____

_____

_____

_____

_____

Joel 2:12-13

_____

_____

_____

_____

_____

_____

_____

Proverbs 19:3

_____

_____

_____

_____

_____

_____

_____

8. Read Proverbs 28:9. In light of this verse, why is it important
    for your adult children to live by God's rules?

_____

_____

_____

_____

How, then, should you pray for your adult children? Write out your answer as a prayer for them.

_____

_____

_____

_____

_____

_____

_____

_____

_____

_____

9. What are three things the Lord has done in *your* life that you could relate to your adult children in a way that would be an encouragement to them and strengthen their faith to believe that God could do great things for *them* as well? In these three examples, include one from the past, one that has happened more recently, and at least one that involves them. Keep in mind that this doesn't have to be perfectly written. These are just notes for you to have when the time is right to share these things with your adult children and they are open to hearing you relate the story. Tell them the great things He has done for *you*, and how He has *changed* you, and *provided* for you, and *set you free*, and how He is *leading* you today. Be specific.

An example of the Lord's goodness to me that happened in
my past is...

_____

_____

_____

_____

_____

_____

_____

_____

An example of the Lord's goodness to me that happened more
recently is...

_____

_____

_____

_____

_____

_____

_____

_____

_____

An example of the Lord's goodness regarding answers to prayer for my adult children is...

_____

_____

_____

_____

_____

_____

_____

10. Pray the prayer on pages 55-56 in the book. What are some specifics you can think of in light of the Scriptures you studied in this chapter—and what your adult child is going through in his or her life—that you would like to include in your prayer? Write them below.

_____

_____

_____

_____

_____

_____

WEEK THREE

Read Chapter 3: "Pray That Your Adult Children
Will Grow in Wisdom, Discernment, and Revelation" from *The Power of Praying for Your Adult Children*

1. According to the title of this chapter, what are the three things
   we must pray that our adult children have?

   1. _____

   2. _____

   3. _____

   According to the first indented paragraph on page 60 in the
   book, list the seven reasons why we must continue to pray for
   those things to be active in their minds and hearts.

   1. It can keep them from being at _____

   _____

   _____

   2. It can prevent them from_____

   _____

   _____

3. It can keep them from either trusting the _____
or failing to trust the _____

_____

4. It can help them to choose a _____

_____

5. It can enable them to foresee _____

_____

_____

6. It can give them a sense of _____

_____

_____

7. It can keep them out of _____
and _____

2. Read James 1:5. How do we gain wisdom?

_____

_____

What will God do in response? _____

_____

_____

Write out a prayer asking God for an outpouring of His Spirit of wisdom on your adult children. Thank Him in advance for the answer to that prayer.

_____

_____

_____

_____

_____

_____

_____

_____

_____

3. Read the following Scriptures. According to each verse, how can a person gain wisdom? Write out your answer as a prayer for your adult children to gain wisdom that way.

Proverbs 9:10

_____

_____

_____

_____

_____

_____

Proverbs 22:17

Proverbs 2:7

Proverbs 11:2

4. Read the following Scriptures. What are the advantages of hav-
    ing wisdom? Write out your answer as a prayer for your adult
    children. (For example, "Lord, I pray that (<u>name of adult child</u>)
    will establish himself (herself) and his (her) home by…")

Proverbs 24:3

_____

_____

_____

_____

Proverbs 3:21-23

_____

_____

_____

_____

Proverbs 3:7-8

_____

_____

_____

_____

Proverbs 3:13-18

_____

_____

_____

_____

_____

_____

Proverbs 24:14

_____

_____

_____

_____

_____

_____

Proverbs 29:3

_____

_____

_____

_____

_____

_____

5. Read Proverbs 2:1-6. Write out a prayer asking God to help your adult children do those things. (For example, "Lord, I pray that You will help (name of adult child) to receive Your Word and treasure Your commands and...")

_____

_____

_____

_____

_____

_____

_____

Read Proverbs 2:7-8. What will God do for your adult children if they live His way?

_____

_____

_____

_____

_____

_____

_____

6. Read the Scriptures below. How does each verse inspire you to pray for your adult children? Write out your answer as a prayer for them below each section of Scripture.

Colossians 1:9-10

_____

_____

_____

_____

_____

_____

Proverbs 29:20

_____

_____

_____

_____

_____

7. The opposite of wisdom is foolishness. The opposite of a "wise person" is a "fool." Read Proverbs 19:3. In light of this verse, what is foolish for anyone to do?

_____

_____

Do you ever feel that your adult child is mad at God for anything that has happened—or has *not* happened? If so, write out a prayer asking God to help your adult child have the wisdom to see how foolish it is to "fret against the Lord." If not, write out a prayer for your adult child to always have the wisdom to not blame God when difficult things happen, but rather to take all concerns to God in prayer.

_____

_____

_____

_____

_____

_____

8. Read Philippians 1:9-11. How does this section of Scripture inspire you to pray for your adult children? Write out a prayer for them using words from these verses in it. (For example, "Lord, I pray that (name of child) will abound in love and discernment so that he (she)…")

_____

_____

_____

_____

_____

_____

_____

9. Read Ephesians 1:15-21. What are the things Paul prays for the Ephesians in these verses that you would like to pray for your adult children? Write out your answer below as your own prayer for them.

_____

_____

_____

_____

_____

_____

_____

_____

10. Pray the prayer on pages 71-72 in the book. What are some ways in which you know your adult children especially need wisdom, discernment, or revelation from God?

_____

_____

_____

_____

_____

_____

_____

_____

_____

WEEK FOUR

Read Chapter 4: "Pray That Your Adult Children
Will Find Freedom, Restoration, and Wholeness"
from *The Power of Praying for Your Adult Children*

1. Read the following Scriptures and answer the question next to
   each one.

   2 Corinthians 3:17: Where is liberty found?

   _____

   _____

   _____

   Romans 8:9: What determines whether we walk in the flesh
   or in the spirit?

   _____

   _____

   _____

   Romans 8:2: What has Jesus done for us?

   _____

   _____

   _____

Galatians 5:13: What have we been called to and why? How are we to serve God?

_____

_____

_____

John 8:36: How certain is our freedom in Christ?

_____

_____

_____

2. Read John 8:31-32. If liberty is a way of life that God wants us to walk in, how can we walk in that freedom Christ has for us?

_____

_____

_____

_____

_____

3. Read Galatians 5:1. How do we stay free once we have been liberated from bondage?

_____

_____

_____

Write out this verse as a prayer for your adult child. (For example, "Lord, I pray that You would help (name of adult child) to be able to stand strong in…")

_____

_____

_____

_____

_____

_____

4. Read Proverbs 28:26. To whom does God bring deliverance? Write out your answer as a prayer for your adult child. (For example, "Lord, I pray that (name of adult child) will not foolishly trust in…")

_____

_____

_____

_____

5. Read Luke 4:18-19. According to verse 18, who needs to be set at liberty?

_____

_____

_____

_____

Can you sense any kind of oppression in your adult child's life? In your life? If so, write out a prayer asking God to deliver you or your adult child or both. If not, write out a prayer asking God to keep you and your adult child free from any oppression that the enemy of your soul would try to put on you.

_____

_____

_____

_____

_____

_____

_____

_____

_____

6. Read Psalm 91:14-16. What are the promises of the Lord in these verses and whom are they for?

_____

_____

_____

_____

_____

_____

_____

Write out these verses as a prayer for your adult child. (For example, "Lord, I pray that (name of adult child) will set his (her) love on You so that You will deliver him (her). And when he (she) calls on Your name, I pray You will...")

_____

_____

_____

_____

_____

_____

7. Read Exodus 20:3-6. Write out a prayer asking God to show you if there is any place in your heart where you have an image in your mind of who your adult children should be or what they should do that is not in alignment with God's will for their lives. (I know this is a hard prayer because we all want the best for our children, but we need to hear from God about this so that we always pray in alignment with His will.)

_____

_____

_____

_____

_____

_____

_____

Do you believe your adult child has an image in his (her) mind of what he (she) needs to live up to that is not of the Lord? If so, write out a prayer asking God to set your adult child free of that. If not, write out a prayer asking God to keep your adult child from ever pursuing something that is not God's will for his (her) life.

_____

_____

_____

_____

_____

_____

8. Is there anything in your life from which you would like the Lord to liberate you? If so, write out a prayer asking God to set you free of it now. If not, write out a prayer asking God to show you if there is anything in your life that He wants you to be free of, and then write down whatever He shows you.

_____

_____

_____

_____

_____

_____

_____

9. Can you think of anything in your adult children's lives you want them to be free of? If so, write out a prayer asking God to set them free from those things. If you can't think of anything you believe they need to be free of, write out a prayer asking God to reveal to you anything you are not seeing about what your adult children need to be free of, or anything they are accepting as inevitable that they don't have to put up with in their lives.

_____

_____

_____

_____

_____

_____

_____

_____

10. Pray the prayer on pages 87-89 in the book. What other thoughts would you like to include that pertain to your adult children's freedom, restoration, and wholeness? Write them out as a prayer below.

_____

_____

_____

_____

_____

WEEK FIVE

Read Chapter 5: "Pray That Your Adult Children
Will Understand God's Purpose for Their Lives"
from *The Power of Praying for Your Adult Children*

1. Do you feel that your adult child has a sense of purpose about
   his or her life? Explain what you see and how you feel you need
   to pray. What do you hope God will do in response to your
   prayers for your adult child?

   _____

   _____

   _____

   _____

   _____

   _____

   _____

   _____

   _____

   _____

   _____

   _____

2. Read Ephesians 4:1. Do you feel that your adult child is headed in the right direction in her (his) life? Do you feel that she (he) is living up to her (his) full potential? Do you believe she (he) is fulfilling the calling God has on her (his) life? Explain.

_____

_____

_____

_____

_____

_____

_____

Write out a prayer asking God to always keep your adult child headed in the right direction, living up to her (his) full potential, and fulfilling the calling God has on her (his) life. (For example, "Lord, I pray that You would help (<u>name of adult child</u>) to walk worthy of the calling...")

_____

_____

_____

_____

_____

_____

3. Read Romans 8:30. Do you feel that your adult child has a sense of being predestined and called? Why or why not?

_____

_____

_____

_____

_____

_____

_____

Write out this verse as a prayer for your adult child. (For example, "Lord, I pray that You would help (name of adult child) to understand and believe that she (he) has been predestined and…")

_____

_____

_____

_____

_____

_____

_____

4. Do you have a sense of who God created your adult children to be? If so, explain. If not, write out a prayer asking God to give you that vision for each child and show you how to pray about it.

_____

_____

_____

_____

_____

_____

_____

_____

Write out a prayer asking God to help each of your adult children become all God created them to be.

_____

_____

_____

_____

_____

_____

_____

_____

5. Read 2 Timothy 1:8-10. According to verse 9, what has God done for us?

    _____

    _____

    _____

    _____

    _____

6. Read Ephesians 1:16-19. After reading these verses, how do you feel inspired to pray for your adult child? Write out a prayer below. (For example, "Lord, I give thanks to You for (<u>name of adult child</u>) and pray that You will give him (her) the Spirit of wisdom and...")

    _____

    _____

    _____

    _____

    _____

    _____

    _____

    _____

    _____

    _____

7. Read 1 John 3:2. We may not know the specifics of what we will be, but we do know that our ultimate destiny is to become conformed to whose image? _____

Write out a prayer asking God to help your adult children to become more like Him every day.

_____

_____

_____

_____

_____

_____

_____

8. Read Psalm 20:4. Write out this verse as a prayer for your adult child. What specific heart's desire does your adult child have that you know of? Include those desires in your prayer. Do you feel that the desires of your adult child's heart line up with the purpose of God for his or her life? If not, ask God to cause your adult child's heart's desire to line up with God's will. If so, ask God to keep that alignment in perfect balance in your adult child's future.

_____

_____

_____

_____

_____

_____

_____

_____

9. Read Romans 11:29. According to this verse, God does not cancel or revoke the gifts He has given us or the calling He has on our lives. Has your adult child ever been discouraged by setbacks that have happened while trying to move into the purpose God has for her (his) life? Have those setbacks caused doubt about what was thought to be her (his) calling or purpose? Explain.

_____

_____

_____

_____

_____

_____

_____

Write out a prayer asking God to protect your adult child from discouragement or doubt with regard to moving toward her (his) calling and purpose.

_____

_____

_____

_____

_____

_____

10. Pray the prayer on pages 100-101 in the book. Write down any specifics you can think of with regard to your adult child's purpose, direction, and calling in life.

_____

_____

_____

_____

_____

_____

_____

_____

_____

_____

WEEK SIX

Read Chapter 6: "Pray That Your Adult Children Will
Work Successfully and Have Financial Stability" from
The Power of Praying for Your Adult Children

1. What are your greatest concerns with regard to your adult child's
   work and finances? What do you believe are your adult child's
   greatest concerns or needs in those areas? Write out your answer
   as a prayer telling God about your concerns and what you want
   Him to do in that regard.

   _____

   _____

   _____

   _____

   _____

   _____

   _____

   _____

   _____

   _____

   _____

2. Read Isaiah 65:22 and Ecclesiastes 3:12-13. In light of what these verses say about our work, how could you pray for your adult child? Write out your answer as a prayer to the Lord. (For example, "Lord, I pray that (<u>name of adult child</u>) will never find himself (herself) working without anything to show for it...")

_____

_____

_____

_____

_____

_____

_____

_____

3. Read the following Scriptures and write a short prayer below each one that is inspired by that Scripture. (For example, "Lord, I pray that my son (daughter, children) will never give place to laziness...")

Ecclesiastes 10:18

_____

_____

_____

_____

_____

Proverbs 1:19

_____

_____

_____

_____

Proverbs 13:4

_____

_____

_____

_____

Proverbs 12:24

_____

_____

_____

_____

Proverbs 21:25

_____

_____

_____

_____

Proverbs 23:21

_____

_____

_____

_____

Ecclesiastes 5:18-20

_____

_____

_____

_____

4. Read Luke 12:29-31. How do these verses inspire you to pray?
    Write out a prayer for your adult child with regard to his (her)
    work in light of these Scriptures. (For example, "Lord, I pray
    that (name of adult child) will not be anxious about…")

_____

_____

_____

_____

_____

_____

_____

_____

5. Read Proverbs 16:3 and Colossians 3:23-24. What do these verses have in common, and how do they inspire you to pray for your adult children? Write out your answers as a prayer. (For example, "Lord, I pray that (<u>name of adult child</u>) will commit his (her) work to You so that…")

_____

_____

_____

_____

_____

_____

6. Read Proverbs 22:29. What is the promise for your adult child in this verse? Write out a prayer for him (her) that is inspired by this verse and your answer to that question.

_____

_____

_____

_____

_____

7. Read the following Scriptures. What does each one speak to you with regard to your adult child's financial situation? Write out a prayer for each of your adult children inspired by each Scripture. (For example, "Lord, I pray that (<u>name of adult child</u>) will always seek You so that he (she) will not…")

Psalm 34:10

_____

_____

_____

_____

Matthew 6:19-21

_____

_____

_____

_____

Psalm 41:1-3

_____

_____

_____

_____

_____

Proverbs 28:27

_____

_____

_____

_____

_____

8. Read Philippians 4:19. Do you believe this verse is true for you? Do you think your adult children believe this for themselves? Write out a prayer asking God to help you and each of your adult children take God at His Word and believe this Scripture wholeheartedly.

_____

_____

_____

_____

_____

_____

_____

9. Read Malachi 3:10. Do you believe your adult children find it easy or difficult to give money to the Lord? Write out your answer as a prayer asking God to help each of your adult children to be givers to the Lord in the way He requires, so that there will be abundant blessings for them. Pray specifically about any ways that they find giving difficult and what you believe the reason is for that.

_____

_____

_____

_____

_____

_____

10. Pray the prayer on pages 114-116 in the book. What specifics regarding your adult children's work or finances would you like to include in your prayers? Write those down below so you will remember to pray about them.

_____

_____

_____

_____

_____

_____

WEEK SEVEN

Read Chapter 7: "Pray That Your Adult Children
Will Have a Sound Mind and a Right Attitude"
from *The Power of Praying for Your Adult Children*

1. What are three things that are true about the mind of a believer?
   (See page 122 in the book.) Write out your answers below, and
   then below each response write out a prayer for your adult children inspired by that truth.

   The first truth is that God gives each of us _____

   _____

   I pray that God will give each of my adult children _____

   _____

   _____

   The second truth is that the enemy wants to _____

   _____

   I pray that the enemy will not be able to _____

   _____

   _____

The third truth is that we have a _____

_____

I pray that my adult child (children) will make the right choice
about _____

_____

_____

_____

2. Read the following Scriptures. What does each one say about
    fear? Write out the answers in your own words. Then below that
    write out a prayer for your adult child based on that Scripture.

    2 Timothy 1:7_____

    _____

    In light of this Scripture, I pray for my adult children that ___

    _____

    _____

    _____

    1 John 4:18 _____

    _____

    In light of this Scripture, I pray for my adult children that ___

    _____

    _____

    _____

Psalm 27:1 _____

_____

In light of this Scripture, I pray for my adult children that ___

_____

_____

_____

Isaiah 41:10 _____

_____

In light of this Scripture, I pray for my adult children that ___

_____

_____

_____

3. Read the following Scriptures. In light of each verse, what would
    be the reason to pray for your adult children to have the fear of
    the Lord? Write out your answer as a prayer to God for them.
    (For example, "I pray for (<u>name of adult child</u>) to have the fear
    of God so that she (he) will…")

    Psalm 103:17

    _____

    _____

    _____

    _____

Psalm 145:19

_____

_____

_____

_____

Proverbs 14:26

_____

_____

_____

_____

Proverbs 19:23

_____

_____

_____

_____

2 Kings 17:39

_____

_____

_____

_____

Psalm 33:18

_____

_____

_____

_____

Proverbs 16:6

_____

_____

_____

_____

Psalm 25:14

_____

_____

_____

_____

Psalm 34:9-10

_____

_____

_____

_____

Proverbs 22:4

_____

_____

_____

_____

_____

Psalm 34:7

_____

_____

_____

_____

4. Read Hebrews 4:12. In light of this verse, why is it important
    to pray for your adult children to be attracted to reading God's
    Word?

_____

_____

_____

_____

_____

_____

_____

5. Read Romans 8:6. In light of this verse, how could you pray for
    your adult child? Write it out as a prayer. (For example, "Lord, I
    pray that (<u>name of adult child</u>) will not be carnally minded...")

    _____

    _____

    _____

    _____

    _____

    _____

    _____

6. Do you ever observe negative emotions in your adult child that
    you would like to see her (him) free of? If so, write out a prayer
    asking God to bring freedom in that area. If not, write out a
    prayer asking God to keep your adult child from being con-
    trolled by negative emotions such as depression, anxiety, pride,
    fear, anger, or self-pity in the future.

    _____

    _____

    _____

    _____

    _____

    _____

    _____

7. Read Romans 12:2. In what ways do you see your adult child conforming to the world? In what ways would you like to see her (him) transformed? Write out your answers to these questions as a prayer for your adult child. (For example, "Lord, I pray that (<u>name of adult child</u>) will not be conformed to this world...") Include specifics in your prayer that relate to each of your adult children.

_____

_____

_____

_____

_____

_____

_____

_____

_____

_____

_____

_____

_____

_____

_____

_____

8. Is your adult child experiencing any torment of the soul that you know of? Is he (she) believing any lies in his (her) mind? Is his (her) attitude more negative than positive? Does he (she) have any mind-set or belief that you feel is wrong or ungodly? If you answered yes to any of these questions, write out a prayer asking God to set your adult child free of all torment and lies of the enemy, and any wrong attitudes, mind-sets, or beliefs. If you answered no to every question, write out a prayer asking God to show you if your adult child is struggling with any negative emotions. Write down what He shows you.

---

9. Read Psalm 145:4. Can you think of ways God has set you free from a wrong attitude or belief, a lie of the enemy to your mind, a negative emotion, or a torment of your soul? If so, write them out below so that you can relate them to your adult children. If you can't think of anything like that, write out a prayer asking God to bring to your mind all the ways He has set your mind and emotions free. Write down what He shows you.

    _____

    _____

    _____

    _____

    _____

    _____

10. Pray the prayer on pages 130-132 in the book. Are there any specifics you want to include with regard to your adult child's mind, emotions, or attitude? Write them below.

    _____

    _____

    _____

    _____

    _____

    _____

    _____

    _____

    _____

WEEK EIGHT

Read Chapter 8: "Pray That Your Adult Children
Will Resist Evil Influences and Destructive Behavior" from *The Power of Praying for Your Adult Children*

1. As I have traveled the country over, I have seen parents in all
    walks of life dealing with adult children who have fallen under
    evil influences. And I am talking about even children who were
    raised in believing families in the church. How much more so is
    it with adult children who have not had godly training or influ-
    ences in their lives? It is epidemic. In this chapter I want to give
    you the ammunition you need to rise up in faith and pray in
    power so your adult children can withstand this assault of evil.
    Look up each of the Scriptures below. Write down what these
    verses speak to your heart with regard to praying for your adult
    children.

    Proverbs 3:5-6

    _____

    _____

    _____

    _____

    _____

    _____

    _____

2 Corinthians 10:4

_____

_____

_____

_____

_____

_____

Psalm 18:2

_____

_____

_____

_____

_____

_____

John 14:13-14

_____

_____

_____

_____

_____

_____

2. If you see your adult child heading down an evil and destructive path, this is not the time to sit by and let them fall into a pit so they can learn a hard lesson. That was for when they were younger and you still had some control over how far they would fall. At this stage in life, the stakes are too high. There is an evil force trying to mold both our young children and our adult children into its image. The enemy has set up a trap to destroy them, but God has given you the power in prayer to see them set free.

    Read the following Scriptures. If you ever feel your adult child is being affected by bad influences or drawn to destructive behavior of any kind, how could you pray in light of these verses? Write out your answer as a prayer below each section of Scripture. (For example, "Lord, I pray that You would…")

    Isaiah 54:13

    _____

    _____

    _____

    _____

    _____

    _____

    _____

Luke 22:31-32

_____

_____

_____

_____

_____

_____

Luke 22:40

_____

_____

_____

_____

_____

_____

John 17:15

_____

_____

_____

_____

_____

_____

Psalm 97:10

_____

_____

_____

_____

_____

_____

3. Do you ever feel your adult child has been taken captive by someone or something? Read the following Scriptures and answer the following questions. What do you see as an encouragement to you in each verse and how does that affect your prayers for your adult child? Write out your answer as a prayer for your adult child. (For example, "Lord, I thank You that You can cause the captives to return to You. I pray that You will cause (name of adult child) to return to You and...")

Jeremiah 46:27

_____

_____

_____

_____

_____

_____

_____

Psalm 32:7

_____

_____

_____

_____

_____

_____

Psalm 18:48

_____

_____

_____

_____

_____

Psalm 37:39-40

_____

_____

_____

_____

_____

4. Read Proverbs 3:11-12. Do you feel your adult child is experienc-
    ing any consequences in her (his) life because of evil influences or
    destructive behavior? In light of these verses, do you believe God
    may have allowed certain things to happen in your adult child's life
    as a means of correction? Write out a prayer below asking God to
    show you, whenever your adult child goes through difficult times,
    whether this is something God is allowing in order to grow her
    (him) up in the things of God, or to correct the path she (he) is on.

    _____

    _____

    _____

    _____

    _____

    _____

    _____

    _____

    _____

    _____

5. Read the "Seven Ways to Pray for Your Adult Child to Resist
    Evil Influences" on pages 141-142 in the book. In light of these
    verses, how could you pray for your adult child? Write out your
    answers on the following pages as a prayer. (For example, "Lord,
    I pray that (<u>name of adult child</u>) will have eyes to see the truth.
    Don't allow her (him) to be blinded by the god of this world...")

2 Corinthians 4:3-4 _____

_____

_____

_____

_____

_____

Isaiah 30:21 _____

_____

_____

_____

_____

Proverbs 2:10-12 _____

_____

_____

_____

_____

Jeremiah 36:3 _____

_____

_____

_____

Ephesians 6:12 _____

_____

_____

_____

_____

_____

Psalm 6:6-9 _____

_____

_____

_____

_____

_____

Psalm 107:20-22 _____

_____

_____

_____

_____

6. What is the promise in each of the Scriptures on the following pages that gives you hope for your adult child's life as well as your own? Why do you especially need that hope for your child?

2 Corinthians 1:9-11

_____

_____

_____

_____

_____

_____

_____

Romans 8:28

_____

_____

_____

_____

_____

_____

Psalm 30:5

_____

_____

_____

_____

_____

_____

2 Chronicles 16:9

_____

_____

_____

_____

_____

_____

7. Read Zechariah 4:6. What was the word of the Lord to Zerub-
    babel about the rebuilding of God's temple? What did God
    want Zerubbabel to know about how it would be built?

    _____

    _____

    _____

    Read the following verse, Zechariah 4:7. What did God prom-
    ise would happen to the obstacle (mighty mountains) facing
    Zerubbabel? _____

    _____

    _____

    The capstone of a building is the highest stone in a building,
    the top stone, peak, pinnacle, high point, or crowning point in
    a structure. What did the Lord instruct Zerubbabel to shout to
    the capstone he would bring forth? _____

    _____

What obstacles do you see in your adult child's life that are lim-
iting what you believe God wants to do in her (his) life? Write
them out below and add a declaration of "grace" to each one.
(For example, "Lord, I speak grace to my daughter's (son's)
destructive habit of...")

_____

_____

_____

_____

_____

_____

_____

_____

_____

8. Read Jeremiah 31:16-17. What is the promise from God in this
   section of Scripture regarding your hard work in prayer for your
   adult children? How do these verses encourage you?

   _____

   _____

We can weep in *prayer* for our adult children, but we don't have
to weep in *despair*. Whether your adult child has walked away
from God and from the way she (he) was raised or not, write
out a prayer below—inspired by the promise in these verses
above—that is intended to either *bring your adult child back* to

God and His ways, or to *prevent her (him) from ever straying* from the Lord and His ways. Don't forget to give thanks and praise to God for that promise for your adult children. If God brought those children He spoke of in the Bible back to their borders, how much more does He want to bring *your* children back to their proper place? Remember, God is the same yesterday, today, and forever.

_____

_____

_____

_____

_____

_____

_____

_____

_____

_____

_____

Read Psalm 126:5-6. In light of these verses, when we sow seeds in passionate prayer and have watered them with our tears of pain, grief, and yearning, what will happen?

_____

_____

Write out a prayer to God about all the great things you want to see happen in each of your adult children. Then thank Him that one day you will rejoice over seeing the answers to your prayers manifested.

_____

_____

_____

_____

_____

_____

_____

_____

_____

_____

_____

_____

_____

_____

_____

_____

_____

_____

_____

_____

9. Read 1 Samuel 12:23. Even when the Israelites had done wrong
    and rejected God's ways, God did not turn His back on them.
    He essentially said, "They have rejected Me, but I am not giv-
    ing up on them." We cannot turn our backs on our adult chil-
    dren, either. We may have to separate ourselves from their
    lifestyle choices so as not to pollute our home and negatively
    affect other family members, but we cannot give up. We may
    be tempted to stop praying for an adult child who has behaved
    terribly, but that is what the enemy wants and what God *doesn't*
    want. We can't let our heart lose touch with God's heart for that
    adult child. We have to continue to pray through every situa-
    tion until we feel released in our spirit to stop. We can't always
    see the answer to each prayer, but God works through them for
    His purposes. Even if you are praying and you see nothing hap-
    pening, or you see things getting worse, or you see even greater
    rebellion, don't stop praying. Samuel said he would not stop
    praying for God's people. According to Samuel's words, what
    have we done when we stop praying?

    _____

    _____

    Do you ever feel like giving up and not praying for any one of
    your adult children because you have waited such a long time
    without an answer to your prayers? If so, write out a prayer
    to God confessing that to Him and asking Him to give you
    renewed hope in His power to work a miracle in your adult
    child's life. If not, write out a prayer thanking God for your
    faith in His Word and the hope He has given you. Ask Him

to keep you from ever getting to the point of wanting to stop praying for any reason.

_____

_____

_____

_____

_____

_____

_____

_____

10. Pray the prayer on pages 153-155 in the book. Are there any other specifics you can think of with regard to how your adult child may face evil influences, or how he or she may struggle to resist behavior that is destructive? List those below and include them in your prayers.

_____

_____

_____

_____

_____

_____

_____

_____

_____

WEEK NINE

Read Chapter 9: "Pray That Your Adult Children
Will Avoid All Sexual Pollution and Temptation"
from *The Power of Praying for Your Adult Children*

1. Read Psalm 24:3-5. What are the qualifications we must have
in order to get close to God? _____

_____

_____

_____

Write out these verses as a prayer for your adult children. (For
example, "Lord, I pray that (<u>name of adult child</u>) will stand in
the holiness of Your presence because he (she) has clean hands
and...")

_____

_____

_____

_____

_____

_____

_____

_____

2. Read Psalm 119:9-11. How do you feel your adult children relate to the Word of God? (For example, with faith, apathy, devotion, etc.) Does the Bible have a great influence on them or not so much? Do they hide the Word in their heart?

_____

_____

_____

_____

_____

_____

Write out these verses as a prayer for your adult children and ask God to give them a greater commitment to reading and obeying His Word. (For example, "Lord, I pray that (<u>name of adult child</u>) will cleanse his (her) ways by living according to Your Word. I pray that he (she) will seek You with his (her) whole heart...")

_____

_____

_____

_____

_____

_____

_____

_____

3. Read Matthew 5:28-29. Are you aware of anything specific in your adult child's life that is inviting sexual pollution or could give place to sexual sin? (For example, videos, DVDs, music, films, Internet sites, television programs, certain people, etc.) If so, write out a prayer asking God to remove all that from his (her) life. If not, ask God to show you any specific danger or threat to your adult child's purity before the Lord that needs to be addressed in prayer.

    _____

    _____

    _____

    _____

    _____

    _____

4. Read the following Scriptures. How does each one inspire you to pray about your adult child? Write out your answers as a prayer for him (her). (For example, "Lord, I pray that You will help (<u>name of adult child</u>) to walk quickly away from all temptation and lust...")

    2 Timothy 2:22

    _____

    _____

    _____

    _____

    _____

    _____

Psalm 139:23-24

_____

_____

_____

_____

_____

_____

Proverbs 4:26-27

_____

_____

_____

_____

_____

Proverbs 11:20-21

_____

_____

_____

_____

_____

Romans 8:8-9

_____

_____

_____

_____

_____

_____

5. Read Ezekiel 14:6 and Proverbs 27:12. In light of these two verses, what do we all need to do with regard to sexual pollution? _____

_____

_____

_____

Write out a prayer for your adult children inspired by these verses. (For example, "Lord, I pray that You would help (<u>name of adult children</u>) to turn away from any idols and keep their eyes from looking at…")

_____

_____

_____

_____

_____

6. Read Proverbs 2:10-12. What are six things to pray about for your adult child in those verses? Write them out as a prayer. (For example, "Lord, I pray that (<u>name of adult child</u>) will have wisdom, and that his (her) heart will be open to receiving godly wisdom from You.")

1. (verse 10) _____

_____

_____

_____

2. _____

_____

_____

_____

3. (verse 11) _____

_____

_____

_____

4. _____

_____

_____

_____

5. (verse 12) _____

_____

_____

_____

6. _____

_____

_____

_____

7. Read Galatians 5:16, 1 Peter 2:11, and 1 Peter 4:2. What is the common theme in these Scriptures? _____

_____

Write out a prayer for your adult children that is inspired by these Scriptures and ask God to set them free from all lust.

_____

_____

_____

_____

_____

_____

_____

_____

8. Read Mark 11:22-24. There is a mountain of perversion and sexual pollution standing as an obstacle against our adult children, and they have to learn to navigate around it. How do the above verses encourage you when praying for your adult children with regard to these issues?

_____

_____

_____

_____

_____

9. What are your greatest fears or concerns for each one of your adult children with regard to sexual pollution or impurity? Write out your answer in a prayer to God, asking Him to protect each one of your adult children from those dangers. (For example, sexual purity, sexual molestation, sexually transmitted diseases, infidelity, out-of-wedlock pregnancy, etc.)

_____

_____

_____

_____

_____

_____

_____

10. Pray the prayer on pages 165-166 in the book. Are there any specifics with regard to your adult children and their exposure to sexual pollution that you want to remember to cover in prayer? Write them down below so they will be a reminder to you.

_____

_____

_____

_____

_____

WEEK TEN

Read Chapter 10: "Pray That Your Adult Children
Will Experience Good Health and God's Healing"
from *The Power of Praying for Your Adult Children*

1. Read the following Scriptures. What was found in each of these people whom Jesus healed that contributed to their healing?

Mark 5:34 _____

_____

Mark 10:52 _____

_____

Luke 17:19 _____

_____

In light of these verses, what would be the most important thing to pray for with regard to your adult children's healing? Write out your answer as a prayer for them.

_____

_____

_____

_____

2.　Read Psalm 103:2-4. What are the four things to be thankful to God for that are listed in these verses? Write out your answer as a prayer of praise and thanksgiving to God. (For example, "Lord, I praise You and thank You that You forgive all…")

1. (verse 3) _____

_____

_____

2. (verse 3) _____

_____

_____

3. (verse 4) _____

_____

_____

4. (verse 4) _____

_____

_____

Write out another prayer, this time for your adult children inspired by this section of Scripture. (For example, "Lord, I pray that (<u>name of adult child</u>) will understand that You are the God who forgives her (him) of all sins…")

1. _____
_____
_____
_____

2. _____
_____
_____
_____

3. _____
_____
_____
_____

4. _____
_____
_____
_____

3. Read the Scriptures below. What is the specific promise God makes in each one?

Exodus 15:26 _____
_____
_____

Jeremiah 30:17 _____

_____

_____

_____

Malachi 4:2 _____

_____

_____

_____

4. Read James 5:14-15. What are you supposed to do for someone who is sick? _____

_____

_____

_____

What will happen when you do those things? _____

_____

_____

_____

5. Read the following Scriptures. In each case, how did healing come about?

Psalm 107:20 _____

_____

_____

John 4:46-53 _____

_____

_____

_____

Luke 4:38-39 _____

_____

_____

_____

Luke 13:10-13 _____

_____

_____

_____

6. Read the following Scriptures. In light of these verses, how
   could someone extend their lives?

   Ecclesiastes 7:17

   _____

   _____

   _____

   _____

   _____

   _____

Isaiah 38:1-6

_____

_____

_____

_____

_____

_____

Psalm 21:4

_____

_____

_____

_____

_____

_____

Write out a prayer inspired by these Scriptures asking God to give your adult children a long and healthy life. Pray that they will never do anything "foolish" or "wicked" that will shorten or destroy their lives in any way.

_____

_____

_____

_____

_____

7. Are there any specific areas of your adult child's health that espe-
    cially concern you? Write out all your concerns as a prayer to
    God. List them specifically and tell Him what you want Him
    to do in response to your prayer.

    _____

    _____

    _____

    _____

    _____

    _____

8. Does your adult child have any health habits—or lack of—that
    you feel could damage her (his) health in the future if they are
    not changed? What do you believe she (he) should be doing
    that is not happening right now? What do you believe she
    (he) should *stop* doing in order to stay healthy? Write out your
    answers as a prayer to God. Be specific about your concerns and
    ask God to enable your adult child to change her (his) ways.

    _____

    _____

    _____

    _____

    _____

    _____

    _____

    _____

9. Read 1 Corinthians 6:19-20. Do you believe that your adult
    child understands that her (his) body is a temple of the Holy
    Spirit? Does she (he) honor that gift from God with the way she
    (he) treats her (his) body? Is there anything you would like to
    see happen differently? Explain.

    _____

    _____

    _____

    _____

    _____

    _____

    _____

    Write out a prayer for your adult children inspired by these
    verses. (For example, "Lord, I pray that (name of adult child)
    will truly understand that her (his) body is the...")

    _____

    _____

    _____

    _____

    _____

    _____

    _____

    _____

10. Pray the prayer on pages 180-181 in the book. What other con-
    cerns come to mind with regard to your adult children's health
    and healing? List them below as a reminder to pray about them.

_____

_____

_____

_____

_____

_____

_____

_____

WEEK ELEVEN

Read Chapter 11: "Pray That Your Adult
Children Will Enjoy a Successful Mar-
riage and Raise Godly Children" from *The
Power of Praying for Your Adult Children*

1. What is your deepest desire right now for your adult child with regard to marriage? (For example, finding the right mate, having a marriage that lasts, healing for a troubled marriage, etc.) Write out those desires as a prayer to God for each adult child.

_____

_____

_____

_____

_____

_____

_____

_____

_____

_____

_____

2. Read the following Scriptures. In light of each one, what are the important qualities to have in order to grow a strong, solid relationship that has marriage potential, or that keeps a marriage strong and together, or helps someone to find reconciliation and healing for a troubled marriage?

1 Corinthians 13:1-3

_____

_____

_____

_____

_____

Mark 11:25

_____

_____

_____

_____

Philippians 2:1-2

_____

_____

_____

_____

1 Peter 5:5

_____

_____

_____

_____

_____

3. In light of the four sections of Scripture in question 2, how could you pray for your adult children? What qualities should you pray for them to have? Write out your answers as a prayer to God.

_____

_____

_____

_____

_____

_____

_____

_____

_____

_____

_____

_____

_____

_____

4. Read James 1:19-20. In light of these verses, how could you pray for your adult children with regard to growing a relationship that has marriage potential, creating a strong marriage, or repairing a marriage that has been damaged? Write out your answer as a prayer for your adult child.

_____

_____

_____

_____

_____

_____

_____

_____

_____

_____

5. Read 2 Corinthians 6:14. In light of this verse, what is the most important thing to pray about with regard to your adult child's mate (or future mate)? _____

_____

Write out a prayer asking God to help your adult child to be married to a strong believer. If he (she) is already married to an unbeliever, pray that his (her) spouse will come to know the Lord and *become* a strong believer. If your adult child is already married to a strong believer, pray that they both will *continue* to grow together in the Lord.

_____

_____

_____

_____

_____

_____

_____

6. Read Galatians 5:22-23. How are these fruits of the Spirit manifesting in your adult child? How are they manifesting in your adult child's mate? If your adult child is not married, how would you like to see them manifest in his (her) future mate? Write out your answer as a prayer to God, listing each fruit of the Spirit specifically. (For example, "Lord, I pray that in (<u>name of adult child</u>) I would see more love, joy, and peace...")

_____

_____

_____

_____

_____

_____

7. Read the following Scriptures. What does each verse suggest your adult child needs to be as a parent? Write out your answer as a prayer asking God to help your adult child become that kind of parent. (For example, "Lord, I pray that (<u>name of adult child</u>) will always see his (her) children as a gift from You and…")

Psalm 127:3

_____

_____

_____

_____

_____

Proverbs 20:7

_____

_____

_____

_____

_____

Ephesians 6:4

_____

_____

_____

_____

_____

Proverbs 23:24

_____

_____

_____

_____

_____

8. Read the "Ten Ways to Pray for Your Grandchildren" on page 193 in the book. Write out a prayer for your grandchildren—the ones you have now and any you will have in the future—inspired by these ten ways to pray. What do you want for your children's children? If you don't have any now, pray first of all that you will be so blessed.

_____

_____

_____

_____

_____

_____

_____

_____

_____

_____

_____

9. Read John 15:7.

What is important for you to do as an intercessor for your adult children? _____

_____

_____

_____

What does Jesus promise will happen when you do that? ____

_____

_____

_____

_____

How is that an encouragement for you when you have been praying for a long time without seeing an answer to your prayers?

_____

_____

_____

_____

_____

_____

_____

What prayers have you prayed for quite a while without seeing any answer? How do you feel about that? Are you discouraged or at peace or somewhere in between? Write out your answer as a prayer to God.

_____

_____

_____

_____

_____

_____

_____

_____

_____

10. Pray the prayer on pages 195-196 in the book. What other specifics do you want to remember to pray about with regard to your adult child's marriage and children? Write them below so you won't forget to include them in your prayers.

_____

_____

_____

_____

_____

_____

_____

WEEK TWELVE

Read Chapter 12: "Pray That Your Adult Children
Will Maintain Strong and Fulfilling Relationships"
from *The Power of Praying for Your Adult Children*

1. Read the following Scriptures. What is the main thought in
    each one? Write out each answer as a prayer for your adult chil-
    dren. (For example, "Lord, I pray that (<u>name of adult child</u>) will
    walk with wise people so that...")

    Proverbs 13:20

    _____

    _____

    _____

    _____

    Psalm 119:63

    _____

    _____

    _____

    _____

    _____

2. Read the following Scriptures. Write out a prayer beside each one inspired by that verse. (For example, "Lord, I pray that (<u>name of adult child</u>) will have good relationships that are free of all bitterness, wrath, anger…")

Ephesians 4:31-32

_____

_____

_____

_____

_____

Matthew 6:15

_____

_____

_____

_____

_____

Colossians 3:12-13

_____

_____

_____

_____

_____

Mark 11:25

_____

_____

_____

_____

1 John 2:11

_____

_____

_____

_____

Luke 17:3-4

_____

_____

_____

_____

Luke 6:37

_____

_____

_____

_____

What one thing do all of the Scriptures above have in common?

_____

3.　Read Hebrews 12:14-15. In light of these verses, how could you pray for your adult child with regard to her (his) relationships? Write out your answer as a prayer. (For example, "Lord, I pray that (<u>name of adult child</u>) will be able to pursue peace in every relationship she (he) has…")

_____

_____

_____

_____

_____

4.　Do you feel that your adult child finds it easy to have good, strong, and lasting relationships, or does she (he) struggle in that area? If your adult child never has a problem in any relationship, write out a prayer asking God to help her (him) continue in that way. If she (he) does struggle in that area, ask God to make changes in her (his) ability to connect well with good people.

_____

_____

_____

_____

_____

5. List below what you believe to be the ten most important relationships in your adult child's life. (For example, father, mother, brother, sister, aunt, uncle, grandfather, grandmother, wife, husband, children, friend, coworker, etc.) Next to each one, write a prayer regarding what you would like to see happen in that relationship.

1. _____

_____

_____

_____

2. _____

_____

_____

_____

3. _____

_____

_____

_____

4. _____

_____

_____

_____

5. _____

_____

_____

_____

6. _____

_____

_____

_____

7. _____

_____

_____

_____

8. _____

_____

_____

_____

9. _____

_____

_____

_____

10. _____

    _____

    _____

    _____

6. Are there any relationships in your adult child's life that you believe are detrimental, outside the will of God, destructive, or holding her (him) back from all God has for her (him)? Write out a prayer asking God to take anyone who is a contributor to that kind of destructive relationship out of your adult child's life. Include any specifics as you feel led. Ask God for His perfect will to be done with regard to that relationship.

_____

_____

_____

_____

_____

_____

_____

_____

7. Read 2 Corinthians 6:14-15. In light of these verses, what is the most important thing that all relationships should have?

_____

_____

Do you feel that the people who comprise the most important relationships in your adult child's life are strong believers? Can you think of anyone in your adult child's life who is not a strong believer? Write out your answer as a prayer for the salvation of anyone in your adult child's close circle of family, friends, and coworkers who are not believers. Bring them by name before the Lord and ask that their eyes be opened to the truth.

_____

_____

_____

_____

_____

_____

_____

_____

_____

_____

_____

_____

_____

_____

_____

_____

_____

_____

8. Read Proverbs 12:26. In light of this Scripture, how should you pray for your adult children's friendships and why?

_____

_____

_____

_____

_____

_____

9. Read Ephesians 6:2-3. Do you believe that each of your adult children honor you? Explain your answer.

_____

_____

_____

_____

_____

_____

Do you believe your adult children honor their other parent?

_____

_____

_____

Because the condition of the parental relationship affects the length and quality of your adult child's life, write out a prayer asking God to help your adult child to always honor you, and her (his) other parent as well, so that she (he) will have a long and prosperous life according to God's Word.

_____

_____

_____

_____

_____

_____

_____

_____

_____

_____

10. Pray the prayer on pages 207-208 in the book. Are there any specifics you want to remember to pray about with regard to your adult children's relationships? Write them below.

_____

_____

_____

_____

_____

_____

WEEK THIRTEEN

Read Chapter 13: "Pray That Your Adult Children Will Be Protected and Survive Tough Times" from *The Power of Praying for Your Adult Children*

1. Read the Scriptures below. Beside each one, answer the following questions: How do these verses encourage you? How do they inspire you to pray for your adult child? Write out your answer to the second question as a prayer. (For example, "Lord, I pray You will be a refuge and a strength for (<u>name of adult child</u>)...")

Psalm 46:1-2

I am encouraged by these verses because _____

_____

_____

_____

_____

The way these verses inspire me to pray is: _____

_____

_____

_____

Psalm 103:2-4

I am encouraged by these verses because _____

_____

_____

_____

_____

The way these verses inspire me to pray is: _____

_____

_____

_____

_____

Psalm 27:1

I am encouraged by this verse because _____

_____

_____

_____

_____

The way this verse inspires me to pray is: _____

_____

_____

_____

_____

Proverbs 2:6-8

I am encouraged by these verses because _____

_____

_____

_____

_____

The way these verses inspire me to pray is: _____

_____

_____

_____

_____

Psalm 91:2-3

I am encouraged by these verses because _____

_____

_____

_____

_____

The way these verses inspire me to pray is: _____

_____

_____

_____

_____

2.   Read the Scriptures below. Beside each one answer the following
     questions: What is the promise for you and your adult children
     in this verse? What do you have to do to receive the promise? In
     light of this verse, how should you pray for your adult children?

Proverbs 29:25

_____

_____

_____

_____

_____

_____

_____

Psalm 91:1-2

_____

_____

_____

_____

_____

_____

_____

Psalm 91:9-10

_____

_____

_____

_____

_____

_____

_____

_____

3. What is your greatest fear for your adult children?

_____

_____

_____

_____

_____

_____

_____

_____

_____

_____

Read Psalm 91:9-16. How do these verses make you feel with regard to God's protection of your adult children?

_____

_____

_____

_____

_____

_____

_____

Write out a prayer of protection for your adult children based on these verses. (For example, "Lord, I pray that (name each of your adult children) will make You their refuge and dwelling place so that no...")

_____

_____

_____

_____

_____

_____

_____

_____

4. Read the following Scriptures. Beside each one answer the following question: What is the encouragement and the promise in this section of Scripture? Write out your answer as a prayer for your adult child. (For example, "Lord, I pray for (<u>name of adult child</u>) and ask that You would be his (her) rock, fortress and deliverer so that he (she) will stand on solid ground and always be protected…")

Psalm 18:2-3

_____

_____

_____

_____

_____

_____

Psalm 34:6

_____

_____

_____

_____

_____

_____

5. Read Psalm 23:4. Why did the psalmist have no fear? _____

_____

Write out a prayer for your adult child asking God to always be with him (her) in even the most troubling of times and dangerous of places. Ask God to enable him (her) to always sense His presence and hand of protection.

_____

_____

_____

_____

_____

_____

_____

_____

_____

_____

6. Read the following Scriptures. What is the promise to you in each one?

Deuteronomy 31:6

_____

_____

_____

_____

_____

Isaiah 41:10

_____

_____

_____

_____

Isaiah 41:13

_____

_____

_____

_____

Write out a prayer for your adult children based on the Scriptures above. (For example, "Lord, I pray that You will help (names of adult children) to be strong and courageous and without fear because...")

_____

_____

_____

_____

_____

_____

_____

_____

7. Read the following Scriptures. How does each one answer to the danger listed above them?

If something embarrassing has happened to you...

Isaiah 50:7

_____

_____

_____

_____

_____

_____

_____

If you are going through troubled times...

Psalm 9:9

_____

_____

_____

_____

_____

_____

_____

_____

_____

If you have a fear of failure…

Jude 24-25

_____

_____

_____

_____

_____

_____

When you need protection from the enemy…

Deuteronomy 33:27

_____

_____

_____

_____

_____

_____

8. Read the following Scriptures. How does each one speak to the dangers of temptation that are all around your adult children? Write out your answers as a prayer. (For example, "Lord, I pray that there will be no temptation that overtakes (<u>name of adult child</u>) that cannot be overcome because You are faithful to…")

1 Corinthians 10:13

_____

_____

_____

_____

_____

_____

2 Peter 2:9

_____

_____

_____

_____

_____

9. Read the following Scriptures. According to each verse, who is given protection by God?

2 Chronicles 16:9

_____

_____

_____

_____

Psalm 72:12

_____

_____

_____

_____

Psalm 145:20

_____

_____

_____

_____

Psalm 37:17

_____

_____

_____

_____

Proverbs 14:26

_____

_____

_____

_____

Isaiah 59:19

_____

_____

_____

_____

Write out a prayer of thanksgiving to God below for all of His promises of protection for you and your adult children.

_____

_____

_____

_____

10. Pray the prayer on pages 226-227 in the book. What other specifics can you think of to include in your prayers for your adult children with regard to their safety?

_____

_____

_____

_____

_____

_____

_____

WEEK FOURTEEN

Read Chapter 14: "Pray That Your Adult Children
Will Recognize Their Need for God" from
The Power of Praying for Your Adult Children

1. Read James 4:1-4. Describe anything you have recognized in the
    world around you that illustrates what this passage in Scripture
    is talking about. Have you understood in your own observa-
    tions that there are individuals, businesses, or groups of people
    who do not welcome the name of Jesus or, worse yet, even for-
    bid it?

_____

_____

_____

_____

_____

_____

_____

_____

_____

_____

_____

_____

2. Read James 4:8. Considering this verse and verses 1-4 above, write out a prayer for your adult children asking God to lead them away from friendship with the anti-Christ spirit in the world and draw them closer to Him. Remember that having "friendship with the world" is not talking about the beautiful world God made or the good people He created. It's talking about a world system that is opposed to God's ways. It's fueled by lust and pride. Our adult children must understand that there is a spiritual war and they are in it. They must make a decision as to *whose side they are on*—God's side or the enemy's side. The enemy prowls the world. God is in the heavenly place. Trying to befriend the world's system and values makes us God's enemy. Even though our adult children work and live in the world, their heart must always be toward God.

_____

_____

_____

_____

_____

_____

_____

_____

_____

_____

_____

_____

_____

3. Read Psalm 119:133-134. Write out these verses as a prayer for your adult children to keep them from the sins of the world that lure them, and to keep them away from ungodly people who try to draw them from God or oppress them because they are believers.

_____

_____

_____

_____

_____

4. Read Psalm 97:10. What are those who love the Lord supposed to do? What will God do for them in return? Write out your answer as a prayer for your adult child. (For example, "Lord, I pray that (<u>name of adult child</u>) would learn to love You and hate...")

_____

_____

_____

_____

_____

Read Psalm 119:92. What are we supposed to do with God's laws? What happens when we don't? Write out this verse as a prayer for yourself. Then write it out as a prayer for your adult child. (For example, "Lord, help <u>(name of adult child)</u> to make Your law her (his)...")

_____

_____

_____

_____

_____

5. Read Psalm 69:1-3. How do these verses illustrate David's dependence on God?

_____

_____

_____

_____

_____

Read Psalm 27:14. In light of this Scripture, what should you pray for your adult children?

_____

_____

_____

_____

6. Read Psalm 61:1-4. Write out a prayer asking that your adult
    child will need God the way David did. (For example, "Lord, I
    pray that (<u>name of adult child</u>) will cry out to You from wher-
    ever she (he) is, and especially when she (he) becomes over-
    whelmed...")

    _____

    _____

    _____

    _____

    _____

    _____

7. Read Psalm 56:8-11. Write out these verses as a prayer. (For
    example, "Lord, help (<u>name of adult child</u>) to understand that
    You know every place she (he) goes and all that she (he) thinks,
    feels, and does because You love her (him). And when she (he)
    looks to You, You will...")

    _____

    _____

    _____

    _____

    _____

    _____

    _____

8. Read Psalm 51:10-11. Write out these verses as a prayer for your adult child. (For example, "Lord, I pray You will create in (<u>name of adult child</u>) a clean heart and…")

_____

_____

_____

_____

_____

9. Read Isaiah 43:6-7. Do you believe God can do all that for you and your children when they walk away from Him? Why or why not? Conclude your answer with a prayer asking God to bring your children back—or closer to Him—from where they are now.

_____

_____

_____

_____

_____

10. Pray the prayer on pages 234-235 in the book. Include specifics regarding your adult children's understanding of their need for God.

WEEK FIFTEEN

Read Chapter 15: "Pray That Your Adult Children
Will Walk into the Future God Has for Them"
from *The Power of Praying for Your Adult Children*

1. Read Jeremiah 29:11-13. What is the promise to you and your
   adult children in these verses?

   _____

   _____

   _____

   _____

   _____

   _____

   What do we have to do in order to secure that promise for our
   lives?

   _____

   _____

   _____

   _____

   _____

   _____

Write out a prayer for your adult child based on this section of Scripture. (For example, "Lord, I thank You that Your thoughts toward (<u>name of adult child</u>) are for peace and not for evil...")

_____

_____

_____

_____

_____

_____

2. Read Isaiah 43:18-19. Are there things in your adult child's past that he (she) needs to be free of and released from so that he (she) can move into the future God has for him (her)? If so, write them out as a prayer to God based on these verses. (For example, "Lord, I pray that (<u>name of adult child</u>) will be able to forget every difficult thing that has happened to him (her), such as...")

_____

_____

_____

_____

_____

_____

_____

_____

3. Read Philippians 3:13-14. This is a letter written by Paul to the Philippians. What did he do?

    _____

    _____

    _____

    Write out a prayer asking God to help your adult child to do that same thing. Be specific.

    _____

    _____

    _____

    _____

    _____

    _____

4. Read the following Scriptures below. Under each one answer the following questions: What is the promise contained in these verses? Who is the promise for?

    Psalm 37:37

    _____

    _____

    _____

    _____

    _____

    _____

Proverbs 4:18

_____

_____

_____

_____

_____

_____

_____

Psalm 145:18-19

_____

_____

_____

_____

_____

_____

5. Read the following Scriptures. What is the promise in each one for you and your adult child? Write out a prayer for your adult child inspired by these verses and giving thanks for the promise in there. (For example, "Lord, I thank You that when we know You, we are a new creation in Christ. I pray for (name of adult child) that...")

2 Corinthians 5:17

_____

_____

_____

_____

_____

_____

Ephesians 4:20-24

_____

_____

_____

_____

_____

6. Read Isaiah 43:19 again. What is the new thing you would like to see the Lord do in your adult child? Write out your answer as a prayer to God.

_____

_____

_____

_____

_____

_____

7. Read Jeremiah 17:7-8. What is the promise to us? Who is the blessing for? What do those promises symbolize to you with regard to your adult child? (For example, that he (she) will be strong and unshakable like a tree...)

_____

_____

_____

_____

_____

Write out a prayer for your adult child asking God to open his (her) eyes to see the truth about the Lord so his (her) faith will grow and he (she) will always have hope in God.

_____

_____

_____

_____

_____

_____

8. Read the following Scriptures. What does each one speak to you about the future? What should you pray that your adult child has?

Romans 5:5

_____

_____

_____

_____

_____

_____

Proverbs 13:12

_____

_____

_____

_____

_____

Lamentations 3:25-26

_____

_____

_____

_____

_____

_____

Psalm 39:7

_____

_____

_____

_____

_____

_____

_____

Psalm 33:18

_____

_____

_____

_____

_____

_____

_____

Romans 15:13

_____

_____

_____

_____

_____

_____

Psalm 119:81

_____

_____

_____

_____

_____

_____

_____

Zechariah 9:12

_____

_____

_____

_____

_____

_____

What is the one word that is common in each of the Scriptures above that we need to have? _____

_____

9. Read the letter to your adult child that is found on pages 240-243 in the book. What other specific things would you like to say to each of your adult children that are not included in that prayer? What words of encouragement would you like to give each one of them specifically? Write them out here and include them in your own letter that you will write to them.

_____

_____

_____

_____

_____

_____

_____

_____

_____

_____

_____

_____

_____

_____

_____

_____

_____

10. Pray the prayer on page 244 in the book. List below some specifics you would like to see happen regarding the future of each of your adult children.

_____

_____

_____

_____

_____

_____

_____

_____

_____

_____

_____

_____

_____

_____

_____

_____

_____

_____

_____

_____

_____

_____

Answers to Prayer

What answers to prayer have you seen since you
started praying for your adult children? Be sure to
write them down. It's important to acknowledge
what God has done and praise Him for it.

_____

_____

_____

_____

_____

_____

_____

_____

_____

_____

_____

_____

_____

_____

Answers to Prayer

_____
_____
_____
_____
_____
_____
_____
_____
_____
_____
_____
_____
_____
_____
_____
_____
_____

Answers to Prayer

Answers to Prayer

Other Books by Stormie Omartian

THE POWER OF A PRAYING® PARENT

Learn how to turn to the Lord and place every detail of your child's life in *His* hands by praying for things such as your child's safety, character development, peer pressure, friends, family relationships, and much more. Discover the joy of being part of God's work in your child's life. You don't have to be a perfect parent. You just need to be a praying parent.

PRAYER WARRIOR

Stormie says, "There is already a war going on around you, and you are in it whether you want to be or not. There is a spiritual war of good and evil—between God and His enemy—and God wants us to stand strong on His side, the side that wins. We win the war when we pray in power because prayer *is* the battle." This book will help you become a powerful prayer warrior who understands the path to victory.

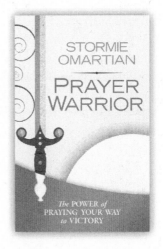

LEAD ME, HOLY SPIRIT

Stormie has written books on prayer that have helped millions of people talk to God. Now she focuses on the Holy Spirit and how He wants you to listen to His gentle leading when He speaks to your heart, soul, and spirit. He wants to help you enter into the relationship with God you yearn for and the wholeness and freedom He has for you. He wants to lead you into a better life than you could ever possibly live without Him.

THE POWER OF A PRAYING® WIFE

Stormie shares how wives can develop a deeper relationship with their husbands by praying for them. With this practical advice on praying for specific areas—including decision-making, fears, spiritual strength, and sexuality—women will discover the fulfilling marriage God intended for them.

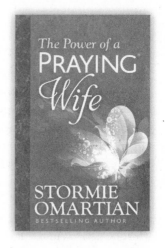

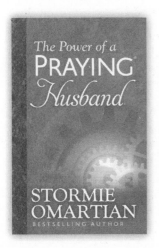

THE POWER OF A PRAYING® HUSBAND

Building on the success of *The Power of a Praying Wife*, Stormie offers this guide to help husbands better understand their wives and pray for them more effectively. Each chapter provides biblical wisdom, insight, and powerful prayers, and the book features comments from well-known Christian men.

JUST ENOUGH LIGHT FOR THE STEP I'M ON

Anyone going through changes or difficult times will appreciate Stormie's honesty, candor, and advice based on the Word of God and her experiences in this book, which is perfect for the pressures of today's world. She covers such topics as "Surviving Disappointment," "Walking in the Midst of the Overwhelming," "Reaching for God's Hand in Time of Loss," and "Maintaining a Passion for the Present" so you can "Move into the Future God Has for You."

To learn more about books by Stormie Omartian
or to read sample chapters, visit our website:

www.harvesthousepublishers.com

HARVEST HOUSE PUBLISHERS
EUGENE, OREGON